We're from Italy

Emma Lynch

Heinemann Library
Chicago, Illinois

Customer Service 888-454-2279
Visit our website at www.heinemannlibrary.com

Editorial: Jilly Attwood, Kate Bellamy, Adam Miller
Design: Ron Kamen, Celia Jones
Picture research: Maria Joannou, Erica Newbery
Photographer: Sharron Lovell
Production: Severine Ribierre

Originated by Ambassador Litho Ltd
Printed and bound in China by South China Printing Company Ltd

09 08 07 06 05
10 9 8 7 6 5 4 3 2 1

Library of Congress Cataloging-in-Publication Data
Lynch, Emma.
   We're from Italy / Emma Lynch.
      p. cm. -- (We're from ...)
   Includes bibliographical references and index.
   ISBN 1-4034-5805-7 (lib. binding-hardcover) -- ISBN 1-4034-5814-6 (pbk.) 1. Italy--Social life and customs--Juvenile literature. 2. Children--Italy--Juvenile literature. 3. Family--Italy--Juvenile literature. I. Title. II. Series: We're from.
   DG451.L96 2005
   945.093--dc22

                                    2005002616

Acknowledgements
The publishers would like to thank the following for permission to reproduce photographs:
Corbis/Royalty Free p. 30c ; Harcourt Education pp. 1, 5a, 5b, 5c, 6a, 6b, 7, 8, 9a, 9b, 10, 11, 12a, 12b, 13a, 13b, 14a, 14b, 15, 16, 17, 18, 19, 20a, 20b, 21a, 21b, 22a, 22b, 23, 24a, 24b, 25, 26a, 26b, 27, 28a, 28b, 29a, 29b, 30b (Sharron Lovell); Photodisc p. 30a.

Cover photograph of Alberto and his friend, reproduced with permission of Harcourt Education Ltd/Sharron Lovell.

Many thanks to Lucia, Sara, Alberto, and their families.

Every effort has been made to contact copyright holders of any material reproduced in this book. Any omissions will be rectified in subsequent printings if notice is given to the publishers.

The paper used to print this book comes from sustainable sources.

Contents

Some words are shown in bold, **like this**. You can find out what they mean by looking in the glossary.

Where Is Italy?

To learn more about Italy, we meet three children who live there. Italy is a country in Europe. Italy is surrounded by the Mediterranean Sea.

Key
● Capital city

North
W — E
S

Venice

Santa Margherita

Pisa

Rome

ITALY

Sardinia

0   50   100   150   200 miles

MEDITERRANEAN SEA

Sicily

EUROPE
ITALY
NORTH AMERICA
ASIA
AFRICA
SOUTH AMERICA
AUSTRALIA

▲ This is a map of Italy. The capital city of Italy is Rome.

Winters are very cold in northern Italy. Summers are very hot in southern Italy. There are **earthquakes** and **volcanoes** in some places in Italy.

Italy has hills and ▶ mountains. It also has flat, low land near the sea.

Meet Lucia

Lucia is six years old. She lives with her mother, father, sister, and brother. Her family live in an apartment in Rome, the capital city of Italy.

Lucia

Lucia's sister

▲ Lucia's father is an **architect**. Her mother is a teacher.

▼ Lucia likes eating spaghetti!

Lucia's mother

Lucia's father

Lucia's sister

Lucia

Lucia's family has a meal together in the evening. Lucia helps by setting the table. On special days they eat fish. Lucia prefers eating cottage cheese or ice cream.

Lucia's Day

Lucia goes to school five days a week. She studies math, Italian, art, music, religion, and English. Lucia likes art because it is messy!

Lucia's mother

Lucia walks to ▶ school with her mother.

▲ For a treat,
Lucia is allowed
an ice cream cone!

After school, Lucia is taken care of by
her mother. Sometimes they go for a
walk around Rome. There are a lot of
interesting places to visit in Rome.

Playtime

When Lucia is not at school, she likes to play. She plays with her brother and sister. The apartment block she lives in has a big garden to play in.

◀ Lucia likes to go swimming and to ride her bike.

Lucia has lots of friends. She likes to play in the park with her friends. Her best friend is Adriana. She and Lucia tell each other jokes.

▼ Lucia likes funny friends who make her laugh.

Historic Buildings

Italy has a very interesting past. Many tourists visit Italy to see its **ancient** landmarks. The Colosseum in Rome was built by the ancient Romans nearly 2,000 years ago.

▼ People used to watch **gladiators** fight at the Colosseum.

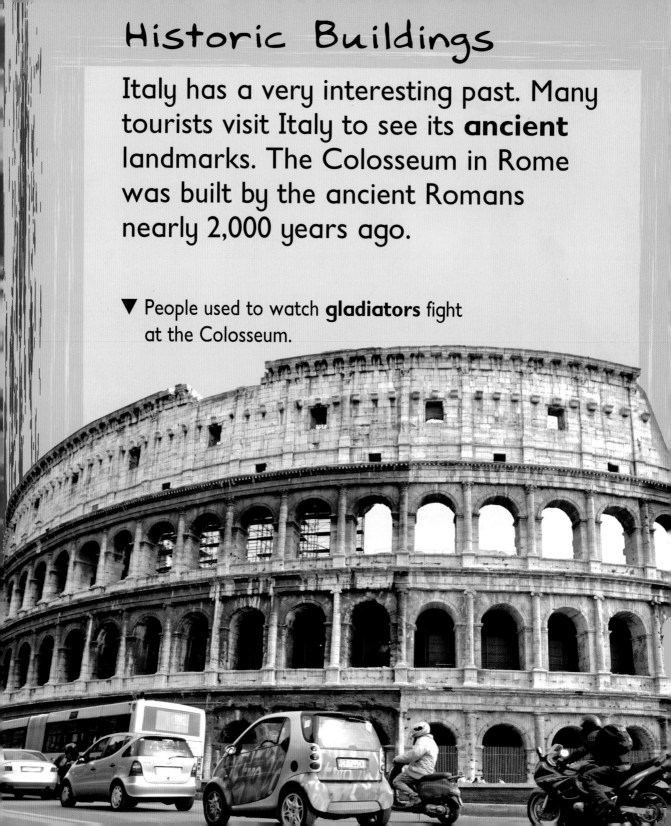

People can walk to the ▶ top of the tower.

The Leaning Tower of Pisa was built about 900 years ago. It took more than 200 years to finish. The tower was built straight but now it leans to one side!

Meet Sara

Sara is seven years old. She lives with her mother, father, and sister. Sara and her family live in Venice. Venice is made up of lots of small islands.

▼ There are lots of **canals** running through Venice.

▼ Sara's father has to work on weekends. Her family tries to spend time together when he is not working.

Sara's mother

Sara's father

Sara

Sara's sister

There are no cars or buses in Venice. People travel by boat. One boat used in Venice is called a **gondola**. Sara's father takes people around Venice in a gondola.

15

Fun in Venice

Sara goes to school five days a week. After school she plays with her sister and her friends. She likes to read books, skate, and ride her bike.

There are no ▶ cars in Venice so it is very safe to skate.

Sometimes Sara and her mother and sister visit her father on his **gondola**. He takes them for trips around the city.

▼ Sara's father wears a **traditional** uniform at work.

Chocolate!

Venice is famous for its pizza and seafood. Sara likes pizza, but she loves eating chocolate. She enjoys making sandwiches with chocolate spread!

▼ Sara's favorite food is chocolate spread!

Sara looks forward to special days and
festivals in the year. Her favorite time
is Easter. She and her sister receive lots
of chocolate Easter eggs.

Making and Growing Things

People in Italy make and grow lots of goods to sell around the world. Venice is famous for its masks. People can watch them being made.

One of the islands in ▶ Venice is called Murano. Murano is famous for the glass that is made there.

▼ Grapes are grown
in vineyards.

▲ Oranges grow
well in
southern Italy.

Different foods grow well in different
parts of Italy. Wheat, grapes, olives,
figs, and oranges all grow in Italy.
There are also fields full of colorful
sunflowers.

21

Meet Alberto

Alberto is eight years old. He lives with his mother, father, and sister in a small town called Santa Margherita. Santa Margherita is near the sea.

◀ Alberto lives a few minutes from the beach.

▼ Alberto's family always eats breakfast together at the weekend.

Alberto

Alberto's mother

Alberto's sister

Alberto's father

Alberto's parents work by helping people who visit Italy on vacation. His father has to work away from home all week. On weekends, the family likes to spend time together.

Alberto's School

Alberto goes to school five days a week. He studies math, Italian, English, art, music, and religion. He likes math and Italian. He really enjoys playing sports.

▼ There are 23 children in Alberto's class.

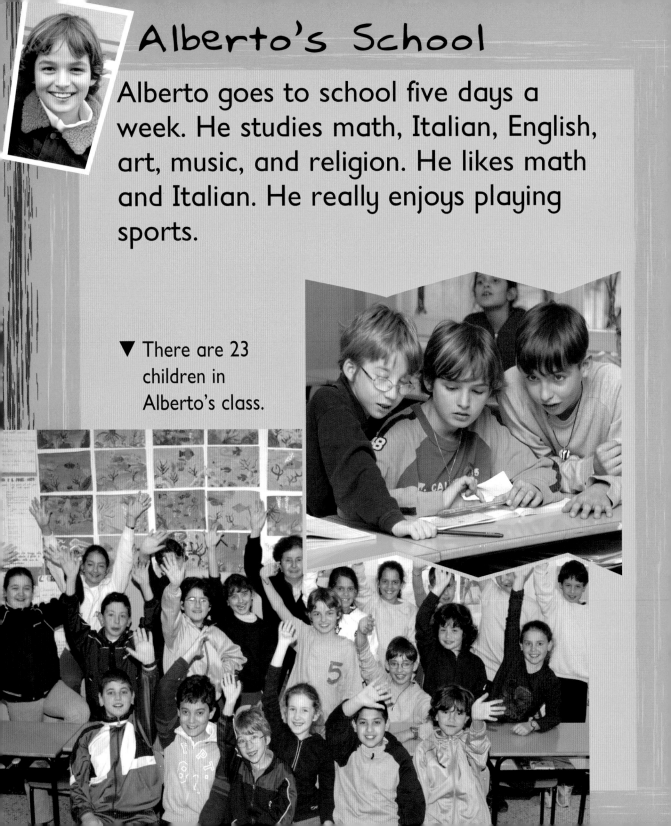

Alberto has many friends. He likes talking to Enrico, and he plays soccer with Lorenzo and Fredrico. His friend Fabio makes him laugh a lot.

After School

After school, Alberto does his homework. When he has finished, he likes to play soccer with his friends in the park. Alberto loves playing outside.

▲ Alberto wants to be a soccer player when he is older.

▼ Alberto sometimes meets his grandmother
when she walks her dog.

Alberto also enjoys swimming and
playing the drums. His grandparents
live nearby, so he sometimes sees
them after school.

27

Food

Italy is known for its tasty food. The markets sell delicious tomatoes and olives. Pizza and pasta are Italian foods. Today, they are eaten all over the world!

▼ Pizzas are made in special pizza ovens.

▲ Pasta comes in
many shapes
and colors!

◀ Italy is famous for its
ice cream.

Many people enjoy seafood caught in
the Mediterranean Sea off Italy. Italy
also has many mouth-watering
desserts such as **tiramisu**.

Italian Fact File

Flag   **Capital city**   **Money**

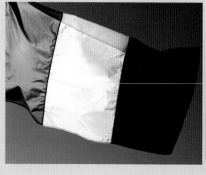  

Rome   Euro

Religion
• Most people in Italy are Roman Catholic Christians. There are also Jews, Muslims, and Protestant Christians.

Language
• Italian is the main language of Italy.

Try speaking Italian!
Ciao! .... *Hi! (or Bye!)*
Come sta? .... *How are you?*
Grazie .... *Thank you.*

Glossary

ancient something that happened or started a long time ago

architect someone who plans and designs new buildings

canal waterway built for special boats

earthquake sudden movement of the ground caused by rocks under the earth

gladiator man who fought other men or animals in ancient Rome

gondola light, flat-bottomed boat pushed along by an oar

festival big celebration for a town or country

plain large, flat, grassy area of land with few trees

tiramisu dessert made of sponge cake, coffee, whipped cream, and soft cheese

traditional something that has been going for a very long time without changing

volcano mountain that has a hole down into the Earth. Sometimes melted rock and ash erupt from it.

More Books to Read

Bell, Rachael. *A Visit to Italy.* Chicago: Heinemann Library, 1999.

Fontes, Justine and Ron Fontes. *A to Z Italy.* Danbury, Conn,: Children's Press, 2004.

Powell, Jillian. *What's it Like to Live in Italy?* Columbus, Ohio: Waterbird Press, 2003.

Index